12 GREAT MOMENTS THAT CHANGED
TV HISTORY

by Lori Fromowitz

12 STORY
LIBRARY

www.12StoryLibrary.com

12-Story Library is an imprint of Peterson Publishing Company and Press Room Editions.

Produced for 12-Story Library by Red Line Editorial

Photographs ©: Dieter Klar/AP Images, cover, 1, 18, 29; Bettmann/Corbis, 5, 7, 8, 15, 28; Stockbyte/Thinkstock, 6; Thinkstock, 10, 14, 26; AP Images, 11, 20; Everett Collection/Shutterstock Images, 12; Corbis, 13; NASA, 16, 17; Dave Bookstaver/AP Images, 19; Library of Congress, 21; Joe Holloway/AP Images, 22; Shutterstock Images, 23, 25, 27; G. Paul Burnett/AP Images, 24

ISBN
978-1-63235-027-5 (hardcover)
978-1-63235-087-9 (paperback)
978-1-62143-068-1 (hosted ebook)

Library of Congress Control Number: 2014946806

Printed in the United States of America
Mankato, MN
October, 2014

Go beyond the book. Get free, up-to-date content on this topic at 12StoryLibrary.com.

TABLE OF CONTENTS

TV MAKES ITS FIRST APPEARANCE IN 1939

Many Americans first watched television at the 1939 World's Fair. The fair displayed new technologies and innovations. Viewers could see inside the RCA company's new television machines. They learned how the TVs worked and saw it was no trick.

The idea for television was not new. The British had been watching TV since 1929. But before the World's Fair, TV was not widely available in the United States. Many fairgoers were seeing television for the first time. They could even view a living

2
Number of TV programs on NBC's earliest schedule, not including films.

- Television had been in development for many years.
- It was given a public showcase at the 1939 World's Fair.
- NBC began broadcasting at the World's Fair.
- TV did not become popular in the United States until after World War II.

THE FIRST PRESIDENT ON TV

President Franklin Roosevelt gave a speech to open the 1939 World's Fair. It was the first time a president appeared on television. President Roosevelt's speech was the first programming NBC broadcast. Now, NBC is one of TV's major networks.

room of the future. Of course, that living room had a TV.

Most Americans did not buy a TV right away. The machines at the fair were expensive. They cost between $200 and $600. Back then, a gallon of milk cost $0.23 and cars approximately $750. A TV was out of reach for many. Then,

World War II (1939–1945) slowed television's growth. Television companies created technology for the war instead. After the war ended, some of this technology was used in new TVs. By the early 1950s, TVs became less expensive. More and more people were watching TV.

NBC cameras film fairgoers at the 1939 World's Fair.

EVERYONE TUNES IN TO *I LOVE LUCY*

Television took shape in the period between the late 1940s and 1960. It was a time of innovation. The period is often called the Golden Age of Television. During this period, many strong programs appeared on television. *I Love Lucy* was one of these shows.

At first, CBS executives worried Americans would not like Lucy and Ricky Ricardo. The Ricardos were the main characters of *I Love Lucy*. Desi Arnaz, who played Ricky, was Cuban. The executives thought Americans would only want to watch other Americans on TV.

Watching television became a popular family pastime in the 1950s.

3

Number of cameras used to film *I Love Lucy*.

- *I Love Lucy* was one of the most post popular shows on TV.
- It was a comedy, but the characters had real problems.
- The show was very popular and influenced how TV was made.

But they were wrong. The show was an instant hit after it premiered on October 15, 1951. Everyone loved Lucy and Ricky.

I Love Lucy was a zany comedy show. Lucy and Ricky got into lots of funny situations with their neighbors. Lucille Ball, who played Lucy, was Arnaz's wife in real life. She believed Americans wanted to see stories about people they could understand. Despite their lightheartedness, she made sure the characters had regular problems.

The show influenced future television programs. Most television shows were filmed in New York. But Lucille and Desi lived in California. They wanted to film near home. Many television shows followed them west. The team pioneered a multi-camera filming technique. They also filmed in front of a live studio audience.

Lucille Ball and Desi Arnaz rehearse on the *I Love Lucy* set.

3

QUIZ SHOW SCANDALS CHANGE TV ADVERTISING

In the mid-1950s, ordinary Americans were winning big on TV game shows. Contestants faced each other in live competitions. Somehow, the audience favorites won frequently. Viewers were

A contestant (right) on the set of *The $64,000 Question* in 1955

$64,000

Amount the top question was worth on the quiz show *The $64,000 Question.*

- Some popular quiz shows were rigged in the 1950s.
- Sponsors and networks made a lot of money from this trick.
- After an investigation, television formatting changed to include commercial blocks.

THINK ABOUT IT

How would you react if you found out your favorite TV game show was rigged? In what ways could the show be rigged? Write three or four sentences to explain your answer.

hooked. The shows' sponsors made a lot of money because many people watched the programs.

But game results were often a trick on the public. Many of the quiz shows were rigged. Winners and losers were determined before a show started. Threatened by its sponsor, a show's producers coached contestants in what to say. This made for exciting shows that increased viewership. This kept sponsors happy. Some upset contestants spilled the secret. The scandal was so serious the government got involved. A committee from the House of

Representatives questioned network executives and contestants.

The rigged shows were not illegal. But President Eisenhower said, "It was a terrible thing to do to the American people." The big quiz shows were pulled from the air for a time. Television sponsorship changed. One sponsor could no longer pay for a whole show. Instead, multiple sponsors bought commercial blocks. They could purchase 15-, 30-, and 60-second commercials. This way, it would be more difficult for a single sponsor to influence a show's producers.

TV HELPS DECIDE THE 1960 PRESIDENTIAL ELECTION

The first televised presidential debate occurred on September 26, 1960. It was between candidates John F. Kennedy and Richard Nixon. Before then, television had not played a big role in national politics. But in 1960, most Americans owned a television. People wanted to see the debates, not just listen to them on the radio.

On a studio stage in Chicago, Illinois, TV proved its power to persuade audiences. Vice President Nixon was well known to Americans. Senator Kennedy was less experienced. Most experts thought Nixon would win the debate.

Indeed, most people who listened to the debate on radio thought Nixon had won. But those who watched

Today, all presidential debates are televised.

THINK ABOUT IT

Today, all presidential debates are shown on television. How candidates appear on stage can play a role in how people feel about them. Ask an adult to help you find a video of a past presidential debate online. What are some similarities between how the candidates appear? What are the differences?

The set of a 1960 presidential debate between John F. Kennedy (left) and Richard Nixon (right).

65-70 million

Number of TV viewers who watched the 1960 Kennedy-Nixon debate.

- The televised debates gave Americans the chance to watch the candidates and listen to them.
- Nixon appeared sickly and uncomfortable while Kennedy seemed healthy and confident.
- Historians say the televised debate helped Kennedy win the election and the presidency.

on television thought different. Nixon was recovering from a knee injury. He did not look well. He also seemed uncomfortable and was sweating. On the other hand, Kennedy was well spoken and confident. He connected well with viewers at home. He talked directly to the camera. Kennedy won the debate. Two weeks later, he also won the presidential election. Historians believe the televised debate influenced this outcome.

TV BECOMES AN IMPORTANT NEWS SOURCE

In the afternoon of November 22, 1963, Americans received terrible news. President John F. Kennedy had been shot in Dallas, Texas. The nation mourned the death of the popular president. President Kennedy's assassination was a turning point for the United States. It was a turning point for television, too.

In 1963, most people considered television entertainment. Most people still depended on the newspaper or the radio for the news. The technology that could bring live news to television was still relatively new. A reporter could not go live with an image quickly. When President Kennedy was killed, reporter Walter Cronkite had to break the story with an audio report.

In 1963, radios were a popular way to get the news.

THE LEE HARVEY OSWALD SHOOTING

Lee Harvey Oswald was the suspected shooter in the Kennedy assassination. While Oswald was being transferred to a county jail, Dallas nightclub owner Jack Ruby shot him. Reporters were at the scene to film Oswald's transfer. The NBC cameras were already on Oswald. The murder aired on live television.

The TV broadcast of Lee Harvey Oswald being transferred to a county jail

4
Number of uninterrupted days of broadcast news of the Kennedy assassination.

- The coverage of Kennedy's assassination made television a major news source.
- Live television technology was new, so Cronkite broke the story with an audio report.
- TV was viewed as a form of entertainment before Kennedy's assassination.

Americans were glued to the TV coverage of Kennedy's death. Television had a unique ability to tell the story of his assassination. It used the power of images to bring the story into people's homes. The story was personal to Americans. They could not turn away from their screens. They kept watching. Networks carried news of Kennedy's assassination without stopping. It began with news that he had been shot. It did not end until the day of his funeral. Kennedy's assassination transformed television into the nation's major source of news.

TV BRINGS WAR INTO AMERICANS' LIVING ROOMS

The Vietnam War (1956–1975) was the first war to be covered on television. Previously, people got news about wars and other overseas events through radio, newspapers, and newsreels. Television allowed civilians to witness the horror of war themselves.

In 1965, large numbers of American soldiers were sent to Vietnam. News reporters followed. They had more freedom than reporters in previous wars. The United States never declared war officially in Vietnam. So, wartime censorship rules did not limit the reporters' stories. For

REPORTING IN A WAR ZONE

Journalists during the Vietnam War worked alongside US soldiers. They often found themselves on the front lines in the midst of battle. They captured the reality of war on film. The images and TV footage were graphic. They disturbed the journalists who captured them. When footage of the Vietnam War aired on television, it angered and saddened viewers, too.

Vietnam was the first war zone Americans saw on television.

the first time, news broadcasts showed combat on television. The invention of color TV made the stories from Vietnam even more powerful.

Wounded newsmen are tended to by US soldiers.

At first, the news was positive. Not much violence was shown. But the Vietnam War was a bloody conflict. As the violence continued, television networks showed more of it to their

3rd

Largest, in size, of the news bureau based in Saigon during the Vietnam War, after New York and Washington, DC.

- Vietnam was the first war to be covered on television.
- Combat footage was shown on television.
- Wartime censorship rules were not in effect.
- Television influenced Americans' views on the war.

viewers. Eventually, public support turned against the war.

President Lyndon Johnson believed television coverage influenced public opinion of the war. It had brought a far-away conflict into American living rooms. Not everyone agreed with Johnson. But television certainly had shown its ability to influence public opinion.

15

PEOPLE WORLDWIDE WATCH THE MOON LANDING

The 1960s were an important decade for television. Many important world events happened between 1960 and 1969. Among them were the assassination of John F. Kennedy and the Vietnam War. One of the most significant events happened in 1969. That year, television viewers watched the first steps on the moon.

US astronaut Neil Armstrong set up a black-and-white camera. This camera filmed Armstrong as he took the first steps on the moon's

Astronaut Buzz Aldrin descends from the *Apollo 11* lunar module.

6.8

Minutes of filmed coverage of Neil Armstrong and Buzz Aldrin planting the American flag on the moon.

- More than 500 million people watched the moon landing on TV.
- Neil Armstrong took the first steps on the moon.
- The astronauts used two cameras to capture TV footage of the moon.
- People all over the world stopped to watch.

surface. Another camera filmed the event from the lunar module. These cameras sent images 250,000 miles (402,000 km) back to Earth. Filming on the moon was not easy. The cameras had to handle extreme temperatures. Temperatures on the moon change from -250° to 250° Fahrenheit (-157° to 121° C). The cameras also had to use energy very efficiently. The moon landing became the most-watched broadcast in the history of television. More than 500 million people around the world tuned in.

Cameras captured astronauts' movements on the moon.

SESAME STREET PROVES TV CAN BE EDUCATIONAL

Joan Ganz Cooney believed she could use TV to teach children. In 1969, she and others created *Sesame Street.* Cooney knew that to be successful, the learning would have to be fun. Characters such as Big Bird and Oscar the Grouch were puppets. But they had human

Bert and Ernie are popular *Sesame Street* characters.

characteristics. Kids thought the puppets were just like them. The show used skits and lots of music. It was funny. All the while, the show gave lessons in numbers and letters.

Sesame Street showed kids living in a city, just like many of the kids who watched it. It became a beloved children's show. Today, *Sesame Street* airs in more than 120 countries. It is shown in many different languages, too.

Children watch the season finale of *Sesame Street* in 1988.

123 ½
The address of Big Bird's nest on *Sesame Street*.

- *Sesame Street* used humor, music, and puppets to teach children.
- It was one of the first educational children's programs.
- *Sesame Street* showed kids who lived in cities, like many of those who watched it.
- Today, versions of *Sesame Street* are shown all over the world.

PUBLIC TELEVISION

Sesame Street is a program on Public Broadcast Service Television (PBS). In 1967, Congress passed the Public Broadcasting Act. It promoted using television to serve the public, not sponsors or advertisers. The law helped launch PBS. The network offers programming for the American people. It airs educational, informational, and children's shows. It also shows programs about the arts and music.

ROOTS TEACHES ADULT AMERICANS US HISTORY

For eight nights in 1977, the miniseries *Roots* captivated Americans. A miniseries is a show broadcast in several parts. *Roots* was based on a historical novel by Alex Haley, an African-American writer. It told the story of Haley's ancestors through several generations. It showed how people were kidnapped from Africa. They were taken to America to be sold as slaves. One of the characters joined the Union Army during the Civil War (1861–1865). He became a free man.

For the first time, the horrors of slavery of were shown on television. Before this, many Americans did not know much about slavery and its beginnings. At first, ABC executives

A scene from the last episode in the *Roots* miniseries, featuring James Earl Jones (left) and Al Freeman, Jr. (right)

worried no one would watch. But they were wrong. The show was very popular. Nearly half of the country watched the final episode. *Roots* helped Americans talk about the history of slavery in America.

When it aired, many cities in the country declared the week "*Roots* Week." The program proved something to TV networks. Americans would watch a TV show portraying black characters as heroes and white characters as villains.

Roots helped to popularize miniseries programs. As of 2007, *Roots* was still one of the most-viewed programs of all time. There had been miniseries before. But *Roots* was the first to air one night after the other, eight straight nights in all. Its mix of fact and fiction helped popularize made-for-TV movies.

100 million

Number of Americans who watched the final episode of *Roots*.

- *Roots* was based on a novel by Alex Haley.
- It brought the story of slavery to television for the first time.
- Americans were captivated by the show.
- *Roots* gave Americans a way to discuss slavery.

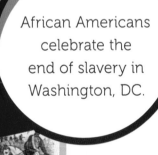

African Americans celebrate the end of slavery in Washington, DC.

10

TED TURNER INVENTS 24-HOUR TV NEWS

On the evening of June 1, 1980, the Cable News Network (CNN) aired its first newscast. Since then, it has never stopped broadcasting the news. CNN was the first 24-hour news network.

Before CNN, the news aired at set times. People planned their evenings around the early- or late-evening newscast. But businessman Ted

Turner wanted to show the news around the clock. He also wanted a station that covered the news in depth. Half-hour nightly news programs could not do this.

To cover news more deeply, Turner created CNN. His idea was not popular right away. But gradually, people tuned into CNN for in-depth news coverage. The station became

The first CNN set in 1980

2 billion

Estimated number of people worldwide who could watch CNN as of 2005.

- CNN's first broadcast was on June 1, 1980.
- It was the first 24-hour news network.
- CNN gradually became a success.
- Now, other stations cover news around the clock.

CNN covered news throughout the day rather than just at night.

a respected news source. News stories were broadcast as they happened. Reporters did not need to wait for evening television. During big stories, people would keep the news on all day.

THINK ABOUT IT

There are many 24-hour news channels today. Interview two adults about their opinions of 24-hour news channels. Ask them how they think these channels have changed news reporting and television.

Ted Turner's new channel changed television. Soon, more 24-hour news channels competed with CNN. These channels felt pressured to cover stories more intensely. Sometimes, this pressure is good. It raises the quality of television news. For example, networks showed more live stories. But newsworthy stories do not always happen around the clock. This led 24-hour news stations to fill time with sensationalized stories. Many argue these shows do not belong on the news.

MTV BRINGS MUSIC VIDEOS TO TV

"Ladies and gentlemen, rock and roll." Those words launched MTV on August 1, 1981. That day, MTV aired its first music video, "Video Killed the Radio Star" by the Buggles, a British band. In a way, the song predicted the future. MTV made television stars out of musicians. TV became important to the music business.

Before MTV, people watched movies starring rock musicians. The videos on MTV were short, usually featuring one song. They combined music and images to create certain feelings in viewers. Often,

1980s pop star Cyndi Lauper celebrates winning an MTV Video Music Award in 1984.

Cable changed the way people watched TV.

the images moved quickly. This style influenced how future television

1

Number of minutes past midnight on August 1, 1981, that the first music video aired on MTV.

- "Video Killed the Radio Star" was the first video on MTV.
- MTV's style was fast-paced.
- The style of MTV influenced future television shows.
- MTV helped increase cable subscriptions.

shows were made. Soon, programs on other channels became faster-paced. Showing a particular feeling became important.

MTV aired on cable, which people had to pay for. When it launched, few people had cable. Those in remote areas bought cable subscriptions to watch television. After the creation of MTV, cable became a way to offer more channel choices to viewers. MTV was very popular with young people. The teenagers who grew up with MTV were called the MTV Generation. They convinced their parents to purchase cable. MTV helped grow subscription cable services.

VCRS MAKE IT POSSIBLE TO RECORD TV SHOWS

The video cassette recorder (VCR) forever changed how people watched television. These machines made it possible to record TV shows to watch later. Before the VCR, viewers could only watch what was playing on TV. The VCR gave people more control. They could choose when to watch their favorite programs.

They could even record shows without being home.

Electronics companies raced to be the first to make a home video player. The machines had to be easy to use. They also had to be affordable. The first VCRs were bulky. Like the first televisions, the first VCRs were too expensive for most people to buy. In 1975, though, the first affordable home model hit stores. It was made by

VCRs played movies and TV recordings off of large tapes.

DVD players became popular in the early 2000s and replaced VCRs.

Sony, a Japanese company. The next year, JVC introduced its VCR model. By the 1980s, many people owned VCRs.

The ability to choose to watch TV at a different time changed viewing habits forever. Soon, new technologies replaced VCRs. DVD technology became popular in the 2000s. TV viewing continued to become more individualized. Today, digital video recorders allow people to record many hours of programming. Internet technology lets people stream television programs online any time they want.

$250

Average cost of a VCR in 1987, down from $2,200 in 1975.

- The first VCRs were bulky and expensive.
- Sony created the first affordable home VCR.
- VCRs gave people control over when they watched TV programs.

FACT SHEET

- Television was formally introduced to the public at the 1939 World's Fair. People learned all about how television worked. At the fair, President Franklin Roosevelt became the first president to be televised. The first television sets had black-and-white pictures. By the mid-1960s, color television was available.

- In the 1950s, television went through an explosion of innovations. Dramas, comedies, and variety shows became popular. *I Love Lucy* pioneered new camera techniques. The show made its star, Lucille Ball, famous around the world.

- In the 1960s, television news proved television could tell powerful stories. Television became the preferred news source. People witnessed televised war footage in their living rooms. It watched the turbulence of the Civil Rights Movement. At the end of the decade, the world watched the first humans land on the moon. Later, CNN would provide round-the-clock news, changing the traditional evening news cycle.

- As more children watched TV, a group of educators wanted to use the technology as a teaching tool. They created *Sesame Street* in 1969. The popular show is still on air more than 40 years later. It is seen in more than 120 nations.

- The miniseries *Roots* became the most-watched entertainment program in history. It started a national discussion about the history of slavery in America. It was enormously popular. More than half the country watched the final episode.

GLOSSARY

assassination
The killing of an important person, especially someone in government.

audio
Relating to sound that is recorded or sent.

broadcast
Sent over television or radio.

censorship
Controlling or stopping speech or communication.

debate
A formal discussion about an issue.

executive
A person in charge of a company.

individualized
Made for a certain person.

innovations
New methods, ideas, or things.

networks
Groups of TV stations that usually broadcast the same programs.

newsreel
A short film that explains the news.

persuade
To cause someone to believe something.

pioneered
To have been the first to do something in a new way.

rigged
Controlled by someone to achieve a certain result.

subscriptions
Fees someone pays to a company to receive a regular service.

zany
Very silly and strange.

FOR MORE INFORMATION

Books

Gikow, Louise A. *123 Sesame Street: A Celebration: 40 Years of Life on the Street.* New York: Black Dog & Leventhal, 2009. Print.

Raum, Elizabeth. *The History of the Television.* Chicago: Heinemann Library, 2008. Print.

Thimmesh, Catherine. *Team Moon: How 400,000 People Landed Apollo 11 on the Moon.* Boston: Houghton Mifflin, 2006. Print.

Websites

The History of Television
www.transition.fcc.gov/cgb/kidszone/history_tv.html

The Moon Landing
www.sciencekids.co.nz/videos/space/moonlanding.html

Television Facts for Kids
www.sciencekids.co.nz/sciencefacts/technology/television.html

INDEX

About the Author

Lori Fromowitz is a writer and editor.
She is completing a clinical fellowship
in speech–language pathology. Lori
studied theater and playwriting at Bard
College. She lives in Massachusetts.